Victoria Art Gallery
Highlights

Interior of the Victoria Art Gallery, 1903
by Hester Quintin Eversley, oil on canvas

Foreword

In financial year 2010/11, the Victoria Art Gallery recorded its highest ever annual attendance figures of 116,000, an endorsement of its policy of involving the local community in all levels of activity, and recognition of its status as the museum most loved and used by local residents. The Gallery is surely a cornerstone of the world class cultural offer that characterises this district.

Late in the 19th century, large numbers of local people got behind the project to build an art gallery for Bath, not only raising the funds to pay for the building, but also giving and bequeathing their works of art to form the permanent collection. Such a groundswell of local support and sense of shared ownership has carried the Victoria Art Gallery forward for the last 115 years, ensuring that it truly is the "people's gallery".

This is also reflected in the nature of the collection, much of which has been donated or bequeathed by public-spirited individuals who wanted to entrust their treasured possessions into public ownership for others to enjoy long after they had gone. Up and down the country, local authorities have been seen as trustworthy guardians of public collections secured for the education, enjoyment and inspiration of their local residents. The splendid exhibition 'Saved for Ever' which coincided with the launch of this book, revealed the personal stories of some of these individuals that lie behind many of the works.

As with all museums, it is not possible to exhibit everything at the same time. Indeed, some works of art need to 'rest' in complete darkness for long periods to preserve their longevity although, like all works in store, they can be seen by appointment. However we are more fortunate than most in being able to make our collections accessible in a variety of ways. Some works hang in other public buildings such as the Guildhall, Pump Room and Assembly Rooms. The Gallery's permanent displays are rotated to keep them fresh and interesting; we hold periodic exhibitions on local themes, invite community groups to curate their own 'People's Shows' from the collection and run an innovative 'Adopt-A-Picture' Scheme in which individuals and businesses sponsor a painting's conservation; this not only gives them the chance to hang it on their wall for a year but puts it in fit condition for everyone to enjoy in future.

We have also taken practical steps to make the Gallery and its collections accessible with the creation of level entry and the installation of a lift to the permanent collection gallery upstairs and the art stores downstairs, where regular behind-the-scenes 'store tours' are led by the curators. Much of the collection can be seen on the Gallery's website, but publications remain an important way of promoting our collections. In the Public Catalogue Foundation's 'Oil Paintings in Public Ownership in Somerset', published in 2008, the Victoria Art Gallery section is by far the largest. This excellent new 'Highlights' publication is yet another way of putting the collection in the public domain. I hope it will inspire everyone to explore the rich and diverse collections the Council holds in trust for the public benefit.

Councillor Cherry Beath
Cabinet Member for
Sustainable Development
Bath and North East Somerset Council

Bath & North East
Somerset Council

Introduction

In 1896, Bath resident Arabella Roxburgh left a sum of almost £10,000 in her will to be spent by the Corporation on a new art gallery. Quiet and unostentatious by nature, she turned out to be a most generous supporter of good causes, including setting up scholarships at Bath's Technical School. George Woodiwiss, Mayor of Bath in 1896, set about raising the additional £4,500 that was needed to cover the costs of construction. This was achieved quite quickly, the fundraising benefiting no doubt from the fact that 1897 was Queen Victoria's Diamond Jubilee. Indeed, Woodiwiss's support ensured that the Gallery became a civic memorial to the Queen, adopting not only her name, but also a regal crown which would be fitted to the top of the building's dome. On 18 October of that year, HRH the Duke of Cambridge came to Bath to lay the foundation stone. Photographs taken at the time show thousands thronging the streets, demonstrating the enormous civic pride that accompanied the establishment of Bath's first purpose-built public art gallery.

The architect was John McKean Brydon (1839-1901), an advocate of classical discipline who had previously designed the side wings of the Guildhall as well as the Concert Room extension to the Pump Room in Bath. The Gallery's location at right angles to the Guildhall meant that Brydon was responsible for more than half of the street frontage along both Bridge Street and the High Street. The site chosen for the Gallery was a sloping one descending towards Pulteney Bridge and the River Avon, the new structure lending an altogether more respectable appearance to what was once a scruffy hinterland of stables and coach houses linked to the White Lion Inn. Brydon's designs for the Gallery included a spacious top-lit picture gallery with a coved ceiling, beneath which was a copy of the Parthenon Frieze donated by the architect. The ground floor was given over to the reference library and print room, whilst the premises immediately next door housed the Technical School, as the art school used to be called. Clearly, the civic aspiration was to create something of a cultural quarter next to the river in this part of Bath, with student artistic practice inspired by direct contact with fine paintings, prints, sculptures and books.

The Bridge Street elevation of the Gallery building included a row of nine niches, which were to be filled with statues of famous artists. Although the budget did not stretch far enough to enable this project to be realised, the women of Bath joined forces to fundraise for a statue of Queen Victoria to be placed in the central niche. In so doing, they took their lead from the example of Arabella Roxburgh, and £400 was duly raised to pay for a Portland stone copy of an approved statue of the Queen. The sculptor was Andrea Carlo Lucchesi (1859-1925), a proponent of the naturalistic and symbolist New Sculpture movement who was of Italian descent but based in London. The statue was duly completed and installed one year after the building opened to the public. The legend below the statue reads: "Erected in loyalty and love by the women of Bath 1901." The Queen had died just three months earlier, whilst Brydon sadly also passed away in May of that year.

At the opening of the Gallery on 29 May 1900, the artist William Blake Richmond expressed a wish that it should honour Bath's greatest painter, Thomas Gainsborough. Whilst the Gallery has indeed done much to further the appreciation and study of Gainsborough's work (see ps. 16-17), the diversity of the rapidly growing collection permitted a broader view, with items ranging in date from the 15th century to the present day. Regular loan exhibitions were held, however, alongside the collection displays, the most ground-breaking being the selection in 1918 of Impressionist paintings from the collection of the famous Davies sisters of Gregynog; this was one of the first occasions a painting by Cézanne had been shown in Britain outside London. The available spaces soon filled to overflowing, however, despite the expansive walls of Brydon's upper gallery. After the lending library moved in during the 1930s, a small extension at the back of the Bridge Street building helped to ease some of the pressure. At the beginning of the Second World War, many of the most valuable paintings were sent to Lacock Abbey for safe keeping. This was a wise precaution for when the Bath Blitz struck in April 1942, Curator Reg Wright, braving the fires that seemed to engulf the city, only had to remove the Walter Sickert paintings that were on loan. With the restoration of peace, future Gallery benefactor Dorothea Henderson was able to write from her home in Bath in February 1946: "I feel so pleased and happy knowing that the things I live with will be housed and cared for in such a lively art gallery and beautiful old city."

Prestigious exhibitions staged by the Gallery included 'A Plan for Bath' in February 1945, setting out Patrick Abercrombie's vision for rebuilding the city in the wake of the 1942 Bath Blitz. A major Gainsborough show was mounted in 1951 to coincide with the Festival of Britain. Around this time Bath was ensured a progressive art scene thanks to the Bath Academy of Art. Eminent tutors such as William Scott and Kenneth Armitage showed at the Victoria Art Gallery in the annual Bath Society of Artists exhibitions, whilst Howard Hodgkin availed himself of the same opportunity to put his work on public display for the first time (1951-53).

The modernist stance adopted by the Academy's teachers and students ensured that the 1950s and 1960s witnessed the most significant flowering of the visual arts locally since the 18th century. Representing this period adequately has been a priority of the Gallery's collecting activity for the last 15 years.

Much the most significant change in the Gallery's fortunes came with the library's move into separate premises in 1989, allowing the Gallery to occupy the entire Bridge Street building for the first time. The ground floor was converted into dedicated spaces for changing exhibitions, whilst the basement was largely given over to improved storage and study facilities. At the same time, Brydon's fine first floor picture gallery was restored to its original late Victorian splendour. In 2008-09, a lift and disabled entrance were added, and the Gallery received a most generous bequest from local residents Lutz and Pamela Haber that included a painting by Paul Klee (p. 48). This bequest paid for new display cases on the first floor as well as drawer cabinets housing the topographical collection. Other recent bequests have included the Derek Manning collection of Victorian drinking glasses that came to the Gallery via the Art Fund. The Friends of the Victoria Art Gallery also acts as a conduit for gifts and is involved at the earliest stage in discussions with donors.

Thus the type of solid community support that founded the Gallery in the 1890s still sustains it in the 21st century.

The laying of the Victoria Art Gallery's foundation stone by HRH the Duke of Cambridge 1897

Statue of Queen Victoria 1901 by Andrea Carlo Lucchesi

The Adoration of the Magi

Circle of Hugo van der Goes about 1420-82
Oil on panel 43 x 72 cm

Given by the Executors of Monsignor James Shepherd 1900

The rich colours, wealth of detail and symmetrical composition of this painting – with the spaces between the figures forming a 'W 'shape – are testimony to the seemingly effortless skill of the artist. Sadly his identity is unknown, but he is thought to have been a follower of the Flemish Renaissance painter, Hugo van der Goes. The picture was presented, appropriately enough, by a monk who taught elocution at the Roman Catholic Prior Park School in Bath.

For many years the painting was regarded as the Gallery's greatest treasure. One young up and coming art historian even suggested that it should be re-housed in London's National Gallery! More recent expertise has decreed, however, that it is not quite good enough to be the work of van der Goes himself. Whoever it is by, it is still a technical tour de force that brilliantly captures one of the most touching moments in the Christmas story.

The subject is from St Matthew's Gospel and shows the Magi, or three Wise Men, offering gifts of gold, incense and perfumed ointment to the newborn Christ child. The Magi were a Persian sacred caste, skilled in astrology and the occult. Following medieval legend, one of them was depicted as black. They appear twice in the picture – on the right hand side on camels, following the Star that led them to Bethlehem, and again on the left, presenting their gifts. The figure to the right of Mary is Joseph.

Despite being the oldest painting in the Gallery's collection, the artist's use of the still relatively new technique of oil painting has ensured that our experience is as immediate as his. During the 15th century, oil paint replaced the older technique of egg tempera, quickly gaining popularity because of its more vibrant and opaque colours which could be applied in layers, thereby allowing mistakes to be painted out.

Death of Cleopatra 1686

By Benedetto Gennari 1633-1715
Oil on canvas 130 x 101 cm

Given by Dr. Charles Coates 1903

Cleopatra was the last Pharaoh of Ancient Egypt. After losing the Battle of Actium to Octavian's forces, her lover Mark Antony committed suicide. Cleopatra took her own life too, killing herself according to tradition by means of an asp bite on 12 August, 30 BC. In this very fine painting Cleopatra is depicted naked, reclining on a sumptuous bed overhung with luxurious red curtains and draped in silk sheets. She supports herself with her left hand whilst using her right hand to put the asp to her breast, which begins to bleed. Her face is averted and her eyes are half-closed as the snake's venom starts to take effect.

Thanks to recent research, this painting is now known to be the work of a significant artist, Benedetto Gennari, whereas it was previously catalogued simply as 'Italian School'. An entry in Gennari's work diary describes it as "a half length picture of Cleopatra feeling the pain of the serpent's venomous bite."

Gennari had trained with Guercino in Bologna but spent much of his life abroad, first in Paris where he received commissions from the French nobility, then in England at the courts of Charles II and James II. His sojourn in England lasted from 1674-88, during which he produced mythological and religious paintings as well as portraits.

Another, earlier version of the Bath picture was painted for Charles II and is now in America. Our version was painted for Francis Gwyn, a public official at the Treasury who had a reputation for being a womaniser before settling down to married life. By presenting Gwyn with his tribute to feminine beauty, enshrined in respectable classical form, Gennari seems to have hoped to receive in return a generous annual stipend. This had been promised, but not delivered, by the late King Charles II.

Ladymead House, Bath about 1730

By an unknown artist
Oil on canvas 68 x 98 cm
Given by the South West Regional Health Authority 1984

This painting has a remarkable history. In 1977 an architect was conducting a survey of Walcot Street in Bath when he discovered this picture in the attic of Ladymead House, then being used as a home for elderly women. He realised that the building in the painting appeared to match the layout of the earliest parts of the house. Although it has been much altered, the house still stands. It was built in the 1680s, but the formal walled garden in front may be even earlier. The lack of any signature or inscription means that the painter's identity remains a mystery. The brushwork, which is characterised by a naïve charm that extends to the inclusion of two smoking chimneys, suggests that this is the work of a provincial artist. He was doubtless commissioned by Ladymead's owner to produce what is effectively a pictorial map of the property, not unlike the engraved views of country estates that were popular at the time.

The picture's re-emergence after 250 years was of great historical interest because images of Bath from this period are exceedingly rare. It gives an idea of how small and rural a settlement Bath was around 1730, before the great period of Georgian expansion and rebuilding. The architect responsible for this dramatic transformation was John Wood the Elder, working to a plan that embraced the whole city and set the tone for what came after. Although on the main approach to the walled city, Ladymead lay outside the main areas being developed and did not feature on the plan, which perhaps explains why the building did duty for a time as a women's prison. All the more remarkable, then, that the painting should have survived, as if determined to confound us with its serene vision. In the foreground, a barge and a sailboat drift down the River Avon, whilst the walled garden is hemmed in by woodland. Within seventy years the area behind the house was completely built up.

The Lichfield Clock before 1748

By an unknown northern European clockmaker and an unknown cabinetmaker
Wood, metal, glass and paint 292 x 72 x 44 cm

Given by the executors of Monsignor James Shepherd 1900

This fascinating musical clock once had pride of place in the private museum of a Doctor Greene, who lived in Lichfield – hence the clock's name – although it was originally made for a church. We know this because the mechanism of chiming bells only plays at church prayer times. The wooden outer case of the clock has been designed and painted to make it look like a stone church tower, with the doors open so as to allow a view of a vaulted interior. Playful illusionism and clever engineering are not, however, allowed to detract from the religious agenda.

The front of the tower is, in fact a 'door' that swings out on hinges, revealing an elaborately decorated clock dripping with liturgical symbols. Four silvered panels are engraved in Latin with the Creed and the Lord's Prayer. Two pedestals project over the clock face, supporting a pair of angels bearing trumpets. Between them is the

pièce de resistance, a 'pavilion' supported by pillars. As the catalogue of Dr Greene's collection dating from 1801 describes: "Within the Pavilion, in the Centre, appears Pontius Pilate, having a Basin of Water before him, as washing his Hands, and round him move continually three Images, neatly carved and painted, representing our Saviour as going to his Crucifixion, the Virgin Mary, and Simon the Cyrenian, bearing the Cross: these three last-mentioned Figures make one Revolution every Minute." The catalogue description continues with a mention of the statue of Fame positioned at the apex of the clock, before concluding with a tribute to the ingenuity of its makers: "The Musical Part of this Clock is very perfect, and executes a Variety of Tunes [including a Minuet by Handel], any one of which it plays several Times over every three Hours."

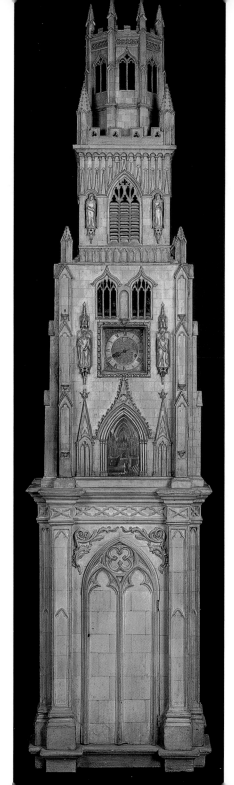

Richard 'Beau' Nash about 1760

By William Hoare 1707-92
Oil on canvas 75 x 61 cm

Given by the artist to Bath Corporation 1762

'Beau' Nash (1674-1761) was a celebrated dandy and leader of fashion in 18th-century Britain. He is best remembered as the Master of Ceremonies in Bath, an unofficial position he held from 1705. He took it upon himself to regulate the behaviour of visitors to the Spa using written as well as verbal decrees. These were displayed in the Pump Room at least by the early 1720s and included a ban on the wearing of swords and on duelling, as well as the instruction "That all Whisperers of Lies and Scandal be taken for their Authors." Nash's strictures, particularly in matters of dress, might seem draconian now, yet this uncrowned 'King of Bath' single-handedly turned what had been a small watering place into a centre of fashionable life. He would meet new arrivals to the city, match ladies with appropriate dancing partners, broker marriages and regulate gambling. By the time he sat for this portrait he was in old age and showing the signs of over-rich living. A notorious gambler, he racked up such large debts that he was forced to move in with his mistress, Juliana Popjoy.

After Nash died in 1761, although the Corporation paid for an elaborate funeral, he was buried in an unmarked pauper's grave. William Hoare, the pre-eminent portrait painter in Bath at the time, presented this painting to the city a year later, intending that it should be hung in the Town Hall. Nash's place in public consciousness was thus assured, whilst Hoare no doubt attracted a few commissions on the back of his gift. His patrons had already included the Duke of Newcastle and the banker Henry Hoare, who created the Italianate gardens at Stourhead in Wiltshire. In 1769, William Hoare was elected a member of the Royal Academy, shortly after its foundation.

An Assembly at the Pump Room, Bath by John Sanders, oil on canvas

Captain William Wade, Master of Ceremonies at Bath 1770-71

By Thomas Gainsborough 1727-88
Oil on canvas 234 x 153 cm

Accepted by HM Government in Lieu of Inheritance Tax, and allocated to Bath in return for a cash contribution raised with the aid of the National Art-Collections Fund (Vera and Aileen Woodroffe Bequest) and the National Heritage Memorial Fund, 1988

Bath's pre-eminence as a place of leisure and recreation is commemorated with this portrait, commissioned by the proprietors of the New Assembly Rooms and is still on view there. As Master of Ceremonies, Wade organised balls, concerts and other social events in the fashionable new rooms in the 'Upper Town'. The picture attracted some criticism when first shown because of Wade's elongated figure and the incongruity of his wearing formal dress in a landscape setting, to which the artist responded by taking the picture back and adding the architectural features. Wade did not escape criticism either, for he had to leave the city in 1777 following an indiscretion with a married noblewoman.

At the time the picture was painted, Gainsborough occupied a studio and exhibition rooms nearby at 17 The Circus. He had moved to Bath from Ipswich in 1759 and stayed for 16 years, a period that coincided with Bath's fashionable heyday. Gainsborough's sitters appreciated his witty conversation and his knack for putting them at their ease. As he settled into his new surroundings, undaunted by the ten members of his family who followed him from East Anglia, his handling of paint became freer. This is evident in the brocading and highlights of Wade's gold satin embroidered waistcoat.

It would appear that Gainsborough tired of the demands made on him by his sitters. In the countryside around Bath he indulged his passion for nature, creating numerous landscape paintings and drawings despite there being no market for such work in Britain at the time. Obliged to continue with portraiture, he grumbled to a friend: "I'm sick of portraits and wish very much to take my Viol da Gam and walk off to some sweet Village where I can paint Landskips ... But these fine ladies & their Tea drinkings, Dancings, Husband huntings &c &c &c will fob me out of the last ten years."

Hilly Wooded Landscape by Thomas Gainsborough, oil on canvas (loan)

Patchbox, Bilston, about 1790-1810, enamelled copper

Christopher Nugent 1772

By James Barry 1741-1806
Oil on canvas 76 x 64 cm
Given by A. E. Burke Nugent 1946

Nugent, an Irish Catholic with a French medical degree, is said to have been a man "who inspired love and respect in all who knew him." As a visitor to Bath in 1756 he met his future son-in-law, the writer Edmund Burke, whose mentor he became. Burke in turn sponsored Barry's artistic education. In this portrait, Nugent is shown in profile with his head inclined and his index finger raised to his chin, contemplating a manuscript held in his other hand. The fact that he is not wearing a wig and there are no precise costume details gives the portrait a timeless appeal, echoing the heads of emperors and philosophers found on Roman coins and antique cameos. This allusion to the Classical world is quite deliberate, for Barry was an enthusiastic participant in the 18th-century revival of Ancient Greece and Rome. Those who could afford it embarked on what became known as the Grand Tour, visiting Italy where they studied the ruins of these once great civilisations, alongside the works of the Renaissance masters. Supported by his fellow Irishman, Edmund Burke, Barry spent nearly five years in Rome, whence he declared in 1769 that "I am forming myself for a history painter."

Barry proved to be a gifted artist with a difficult temperament: he was the only artist ever to be expelled from the Royal Academy. His 'magnus opus' comprised six mural-scale paintings on *The Progress of Human Culture*, created between 1777 and 1784 for the Great Room of the Royal Society of Arts. In the context of such ambitious compositions, one would be forgiven for thinking that Barry might undertake a portrait for light relief. And yet relatively few portraits survive from his hand. The Nugent likeness can be seen as a tribute to the warm relations he enjoyed with the entire Burke family.

The Royal Crescent, Bath 1777

Thomas Malton 1748-1804
Watercolour 33 x 59 cm

Given by Robert Nesham 1904

This painting is a view of the Royal Crescent from the south-east. One of Bath's architectural set pieces, the crescent was built in 1767-75 by John Wood the Younger, possibly working to an idea originally devised by his architect father. Although the name 'crescent' carries Druidic allusions to the shape of the new moon, in plan the curving terrace of 30 houses actually forms a half-ellipse. The elevated site, originally on the edge of the city, ensured that every resident of the Crescent was able to enjoy a view of the countryside. Malton's watercolour typically adds human interest to the scene in the form of a young family, several fashionable promenaders, a couple of dogs, and a coach with its horses unbridled for rest and grazing. The figures are as painstakingly rendered as the architecture, whilst also serving to demonstrate the buildings' impressive scale.

Malton came from a family of view painters and excelled, like them, at meticulously precise city-scapes. In London he taught perspective and drawing to the young J.M.W. Turner, among others, whose debt to Malton was apparent in his early watercolours (see p. 29). Between 1769 and 1788, Malton intermittently made paintings, drawings and prints of Bath, besides lecturing on perspective at the Queen's Head Tavern in the city. He lived and exhibited his work at a house in Orchard Street near the original theatre. Malton's *Views of Bath* can be seen as a unique record of Bath's appearance in the late 18th century, when building activity was at its height. Half of the fourteen *Views* that he made are preserved in the Gallery's collection.

The completion of The Royal Crescent, Bath about 1769 by Thomas Malton, watercolour

Charles Dumergue about 1780

By Johann Zoffany 1733-1810
Oil on canvas 76 x 64 cm
Given by Olive Green 1976

Charles Dumergue (1739-1814) qualified as a surgeon-dentist in an age when French dentistry was far superior to British. He brought his young daughter, Antoinette-Adelaide, who was always known as Sophia, to London in 1769 or 1770. His connection with the Royal family began in the 1770s and culminated in his appointment as Dentist to the Prince of Wales in 1785. He raised his daughter on his own and was also a good friend to eminent contemporaries such as Sir Walter Scott.

Dumergue befriended Zoffany, shortly after the latter's return to London from Italy in 1778, and he would act as one of the executors of the artist's will. Zoffany's personal history paralleled that of his friend, except that he had left Germany behind rather than France. He too quickly found favour with the Royal family, especially with his compatriot Queen Charlotte whose patronage resulted in a group of remarkably informal Royal portraits and group portraits. The high finish and careful attention to detail that secured Zoffany's reputation are supremely evident in this pair of portraits. Sophia, who is said to have been literary and musical in her tastes, loved to give concerts, kept house for her father and never married. She is portrayed here aged twelve or thirteen, holding her favourite cat and wearing a magnificent white silk hat. Her father is also finely attired, his red coat presumably marking his position at the royal court.

Sophia Dumergue about 1780

By Johann Zoffany 1733-1810
Oil on panel 76 x 62 cm

Bought by Private Treaty Sale with the aid of the Art Fund, the MLA / V&A Purchase Grant Fund and the Friends of the Victoria Art Gallery, 1998

Anxiety: head of a young girl about 1790

By Jean-Baptiste Greuze 1725-1805
Oil on canvas 49 x 38 cm
Given by Miss D. Skrine 1951

Greuze has been credited with extending the emotional range of painting, in an age that was interested in exploring new areas of feeling. He first attracted notice in 1755 when he exhibited his picture of *A father reading the Bible* to his children at the Paris Salon. Similarly sentimental scenes of everyday life won him enormous popularity, and his work was praised by Diderot as 'morality in paint'. However, his attempt to gain official recognition in France by election to the French Academy backfired when he submitted a Roman history painting to the Salon in 1769. His humiliating rejection stemmed largely, it seems, from his excessive vanity, which antagonised everyone, his fellow artists included. Henceforth he would only exhibit his work privately.

Greuze achieved fame thanks largely to the popularity of engraved copies of his paintings. Much of the income generated was, however, embezzled by his wife, a former model whose extravagance and infidelity caused him much hardship. After the French Revolution of 1789 he endured poverty and neglect, relieved by an occasional commission from Napoleon and his circle. His death went unnoticed by the art world, which had found new heroes in artists who revived the Classical style. This simple head and shoulders portrait of a girl was conceived by Greuze as one of his 'Expression Studies', depictions of human heads in poses of heightened emotion. Throughout his career Greuze produced hundreds of heads, mainly those of young women, old men and children. Some, though not all, of these heads were given titles that referred to a particular passion. This example dating from around 1790 was clearly intended as a study of anxiety, as is confirmed by the model's frown and distracted stare. The mismatch between the emotion and the age of the young girl only serves to heighten the psychological tension.

A storm with smugglers landing 1791

By Philippe Jacques de Loutherbourg 1740-1812

Oil on canvas 115 x 165 cm

Purchased 1929

De Loutherbourg was born in Strasbourg and moved to Paris in 1755. He was elected to the French Academy in 1766, only to be 'discovered' in Paris five years later by the actor David Garrick. The latter invited him to London and offered him a job as principal scenery painter at Drury Lane Theatre, where he was paid the unprecedented salary of £500. De Loutherbourg revolutionised stage scenery in England, mainly though his use of variously shaped 'flats' painted with picturesque scenes that were lit from behind through gauzes. His adept handling of light effects and elemental forces, heightened for dramatic effect, were also brought into play for the purposes of his Eidophusikon, which he invented in 1782. This was an early type of magic lantern that relied on shifting scenes, its early devotees including Gainsborough and Joshua Reynolds.

When de Loutherbourg was not busy creating optical illusions, he was a successful landscape painter who exhibited frequently at the Royal Academy. In his whole-hearted commitment to the Sublime, he earned the esteem of the young Turner, who would surely have appreciated the battle between man and nature that is acted out in *A storm with smugglers landing*. Rather than being an accurate depiction of a real place, the painting is a product of the artist's imagination. It was purchased by the Gallery from the estate of Alfred Jones, a well-known Bath picture dealer. After his death in 1928 he was praised in an obituary in the *Bath Chronicle*: "Mr Jones was an Irishman – brilliant, witty, and in great demand whenever people of culture met." Over the years, Jones presented several hundred pictures to the Gallery and became one of its most significant benefactors.

The west front of Bath Abbey 1796

By Joseph Mallord William Turner 1775-1851

Watercolour 24 x 29 cm

Purchased with the aid of the MLA / V&A Purchase Grant Fund, the Art Fund and the Friends of the Victoria Art Gallery, 1994

Turner, the son of a Covent Garden barber, was a child prodigy. He entered the Royal Academy Schools to study art aged 14 and exhibited this watercolour at the Academy in 1796 when he was just 21. He first visited Bath in 1791 when undertaking one of his tours of the West Country. These took in sites with picturesque Gothic buildings like Bath Abbey, as well as ruins such as Tintern and Glastonbury. Turner owed his ability to render the detail of buildings accurately to his earlier training under Thomas Malton (see p. 20), an architectural view painter whom he later described as "my real master."

Malton's example would doubtless have encouraged Turner to enliven his foreground with figures in contemporary dress, going about their everyday business. These include two men standing next to a sedan chair, holding the door open in the hope of attracting trade from the lady in white crossing the churchyard from the left. When Turner painted this view, there were still 17th- and 18th-century houses abutting the north and south facades of the church, some of them incorporating shops. These houses were demolished in the 1820s, as was the house just visible to the right of the picture which had been Gainsborough's first studio in Bath. Turner has ensured that the Abbey itself is lit up by a radiant beam of light, as if to recall the dream that inspired the decoration of this part of the church. After visiting the Abbey's Norman precursor in 1499 and being distressed by its dilapidated state, Oliver King, the Bishop of Bath and Wells, had a dream in which angels descended from heaven on ladders. They instructed him to build the church and are commemorated in stone, running up and down ladders to either side of the Abbey's great west window.

Patchbox, Bilston, about 1790-1810, enamelled copper

Comforts of Bath: the doctors 1790s

By Thomas Rowlandson 1756-1827
Pen and watercolour 13 x 19 cm
Purchased 1943

In the 1790s, the social profile of visitors to Bath was changing, from the former predominantly aristocratic clientele to tourists from the lower classes. Caricaturists like Nixon and Rowlandson were quick to satirise this new breed of visitor, even comparing notes when they travelled together and when they both visited Bath in 1792. Six years later Rowlandson published his observations as a suite of twelve prints entitled *The Comforts of Bath*, each one dedicated to an essential activity of a visitor to the Spa: going to a ball, taking the waters, gambling and eating good food. His caustic wit spared nobody, whatever their infirmity or propensity to misbehave. During this period Bath was a honey pot for doctors as well as quacks, responding to the demand created by the huge numbers of invalids attending the Spa in the hope of a cure. Rowlandson here shows doctors administering to an overweight, gouty patient, like vultures gathered around a wounded beast.

The patient certainly looks incapable of voluntary immersion in the thermal waters, unlike the bathers in John Nixon's *The King's Bath*, although they too are not spared the caricaturist's biting satire. Some of Nixon's bathers seem to be expiring from the heat or the overcrowding, whilst others leer at their companions. Clearly there was little if any privacy for those taking the waters, bearing in mind the proximity of the adjacent buildings. Add to this the lack of any protection from the weather, and it will come as no surprise that the King's and Queen's Baths were regarded as uncivilised and insanitary by the late 18th century. Nixon's bathers are, somewhat ironically, presided over by a statue of Bladud who, legend has it, discovered the healing properties of the natural spring after his swine emerged from the waters cured of their skin diseases.

The King's Bath, Bath 1800

By John Nixon about 1750-1818
Pen and watercolour 31 x 41 cm
Given by Reverend A.E. Hunt 1918

The Bride in Death 1839

By Thomas Jones Barker 1813-82
Oil on canvas 125 x 167 cm

Given by Alderman Cedric Chivers 1923

Thomas Jones Barker was the eldest son of the Bath-based painter, Thomas Barker. The latter came to notice by setting up the first lithographic printing press outside London in 1813, while visitors to his Neoclassical home were awestruck by his murals depicting scenes from the Greek War of Independence. The young Thomas Jones, however, felt the need to develop his own style of painting away from Bath. After studying in Paris with the French painter Horace Vernet, he had a successful career working in London and Paris. He painted *The Bride in Death* for Princess Marie, the youngest daughter of King Louis Philippe of France. It is Barker's most famous painting and he won prizes and medals for it in France. The story it tells is, however, a sad one. A young woman has died on the eve of her wedding and lies mourned by the man she was about to marry.

The picture was inspired by an anonymous ballad, one verse of which is visible on a scroll that can be seen on the bedside table to the left:

But place the violets in her hand
And o'er her brows a cypress band
And look your last on her pretty face
Ere she goes to her latest resting place.

Many of the objects in the painting have been chosen for their symbolic meanings. The hourglass beside the bed represents the passing of time and the shortness of life. The violets in the woman's hand signify sadness, while her white clothes and pearls emphasise her purity. And to the right of the picture, beside the grief-stricken man, the dog symbolises loyalty and devotion.

Rustic Figure 1813
by Thomas Barker,
lithographic stone

Going to the hayfield 1852

By David Cox 1783-1859
Oil on board 28 x 37 cm
Given by F.J. Nettlefold 1948

The freshness of the brushwork in this little picture seems remarkable considering it is over 150 years old, and the word Impressionism would not be coined for another 22 years. We can feel the wind catching the skirts of the women and the tail of the horse, whilst the shadows of the passing clouds are captured with telling observation in the hayfield. Cox was 69 when he painted this picture, using oil paint rather than his customary medium which was watercolour. Defying convention, he ensured that his watercolours also had a rough tooth, for he loved to splash the colour about and let it settle into the nooks and crannies of the Scotch wrapping paper that he painted on for much of his life. He made many sketching tours of England and Wales, besides publishing several treatises on landscape painting and working as a drawing master.

It was only in 1840 that he began to use oil paint seriously, taking lessons from the Bristol painter William James Müller, who was then half his own age.

There are no fewer than fifteen versions of *Going to the hayfield*, for it was Cox's most popular subject by far. Although the essential elements remained constant – a mounted countryman, usually with a dog, heading for the hayfield – the artist took pains to avoid actual repetition, inserting additional figures and trees (as here), or a gate. But this being the Victorian period, Cox does not fail to suggest a bit of a story: the man on horseback is carrying a basket on his arm, quite possibly containing lunch which he is taking to the hungry workers scything hay in the middle distance. The grass is so high that the harvesters' legs are invisible, like those of the team of horses hitched to the haycart.

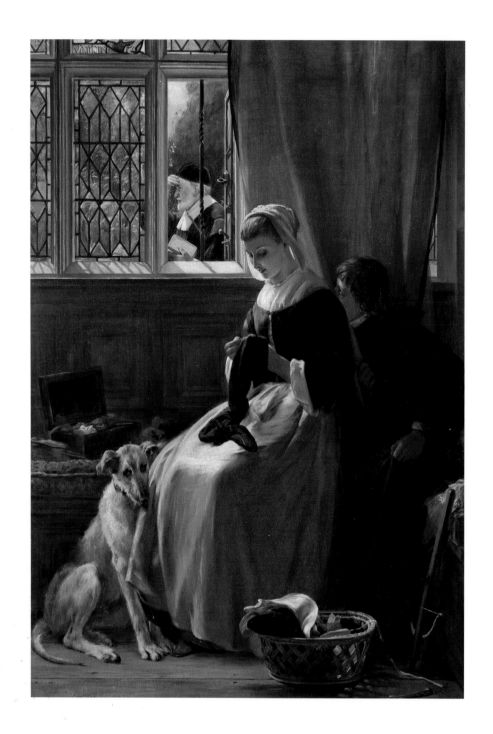

The truant in hiding 1870

By John Callcott Horsley 1817-1903
Oil on canvas 100 x 73 cm

Bequeathed by Alice Dorothea Henderson 1954

Horsley was a successful painter of historical and contemporary narrative pictures. From 1875-90 he served as Rector of the Royal Academy, where his prudish objection to the painting of nude models earned him the nickname 'Clothes-Horsley'. His main claim to fame is that he designed the first ever commercial Christmas card in 1843, although it caused some controversy for including the figure of a child drinking wine. His sister married the engineer Isambard Kingdom Brunel, who became a lifelong friend of the artist, which is ironic considering Horsley's unwillingness to confront industrial progress.

Horsley lived at Willesley House in Cranbrook, a small medieval town in Kent that attracted a colony of artists made up of close friends and relatives. Willesley, a brick house dating back to the 18th century, was enlarged by Horsley in 1864-65, using Richard Shaw as architect.

The additions included some mock Tudor timbering and leaded light windows, which are visible in the background of *The truant in hiding*. The figure of the maid was modelled by Miss Emily Kennard, the 19-year old daughter of the local carpenter and undertaker. She modelled on several occasions for Horsley, who varied her costume and social status in another painting where she appears as a fashionable young lady visiting her banker. The artist must have been able to draw on a considerable supply of props to create the desired historical ambience for each picture. Like most of Horsley's paintings, this one tells a story and has been set in the 17th century. The boy has run away from his lessons and now hides behind the maid as his angry tutor searches for him in the garden. The maid's covert sideways glance shows that she sympathises with the boy and will not give his whereabouts away.

Golgotha about 1884

By Mihály Munkácsy 1844-1900

Oil on canvas 117 x 170 cm

Given by Mary English 1919

This painting has two amazing stories to tell, one of its making and the other of how it ended up in Bath. The Hungarian Munkácsy shot to international fame after winning a gold medal at the 1870 Paris Salon and then signing a contract with the art dealer Charles Sedelmeyer. The latter decided to promote Munkácsy worldwide, aided by three huge pictures dedicated to the passion of Christ. After exhaustive and lengthy preparations, *Christ before Pilate* was finished in 1881, *Golgotha* in 1884 and *Ecce Homo* in 1896. Each of the completed paintings measured more than four metres by six metres and was toured around Europe and America. People flocked in their tens of thousands to see the pictures, mesmerised by their sheer scale. The first two parts of the trilogy were bought in 1887-88 by the millionaire, John Wanamaker for 335,000 dollars and exhibited in his Philadelphia mansion and later his department store.

This large-scale study for *Golgotha*, Munkácsy's interpretation of the Crucifixion, leaves a strong impression owing to the vivid expressions of the bystanders and the use of dramatic lighting. While the full size version was underway, the man modelling for the figure of Christ fell off his pedestal and was injured. The artist promptly had himself strapped to the cross and photographed, the better to appreciate what it felt like to be crucified.

Thirty years later, the picture acquired added poignancy due to its connection with a more recent atrocity. It was given to the Gallery in 1919 by Mary English, "in memory of my son Captain Robert E. English and others of the North Somerset Yeomanry who have fallen in this terrible war." Robert had been killed at the Second Battles of Ypres on May 13, 1915. His mother, who lived in London, chose a Bath gallery as recipient for her gift because the Yeomanry had been based in the city.

Portrait of Anna Bilinska 1886

By Emmeline Deane 1858-1944

Oil on canvas 128 x 91 cm

Given by Helen Lavinia Cochrane 1945

A young female art student from Britain paints another female art student from Poland; the setting is Paris, the date the mid-1880s. Even without knowing all this, one can still sense in this picture a coming together of two adventurous spirits, eager to overstep the conventional bounds of language, geography and sexual stereotyping. The sitter for this arresting portrait was the Polish artist Anna Bilinska (1857-93), who had enrolled at the Académie Julian in Paris in 1882. The official French art academy did not admit women at this time, and Julian was quick to spy an opportunity, one of his American pupils noting that "women flocked thither from all parts of the world, but they divided honors [sic] with the men." Anna is depicted in mourning dress, her father having died in 1884 and her fiancé a year later. In order to regain her health after suffering a nervous breakdown, Anna travelled round France, painting landscapes whilst staying with friends.

On her return to Paris in 1886, Rodolphe Julian appointed her head of an academic studio. After marrying in 1892, she was planning to establish an art school for women in Warsaw, but died tragically young of heart disease.

Emmeline Deane, who came from Bath, probably met and befriended Anna at Julian's Académie in Paris, where her family had sent her in the interest of improving her artistic education. Emmeline succeeded in exhibiting her portrait of Anna at the Paris Salon of 1886 and again at London's Royal Academy a year later, where its profound melancholy caused a stir and was even caricatured in *Punch*. Emmeline never parted with the portrait. She went on to become a portraitist and miniaturist, exhibiting seven times at the Royal Academy and famously managing to secure a sitting from Cardinal John Newman. Sadly much of her work was destroyed in the London Blitz.

Saint Elizabeth and Saint Dorothea 1895

By George Frampton 1860-1928

Oil on panel with stained leather, silk brocade, semi-precious stones, mother of pearl and ivory; painted panels each 96 x 36 cm

Given by Alice Dorothea Henderson 1954

The Arts and Craft Movement is known for its beautiful but functional furniture and decorative objects, made by hand in reaction against the proliferation of cheap, industrially produced items. These two paintings are part of a four-panel folding fire-screen that also features a rose tree and an apple tree. Above the image of St Elizabeth of Hungary is the inscription: "And in her lap there lay the red and white roses of Paradise", referring to the food the saint was carrying to the poor which turned to roses when she was stopped by her enraged husband. The legend above St Dorothea reads: "In his garden grow celestial fruits and roses that never fade", alluding to her promise to a scoffing bystander, when on the way to her death, that she would confirm her arrival in paradise by sending him apples.

George Frampton was a leading figure in the Arts and Crafts Movement and a member of the Art Workers' Guild. He is probably best known for his statue of Peter Pan in Kensington Gardens, London, although the screen is a highly significant early work. It was reproduced in *Studio* magazine in 1896 and given special mention in the *Magazine of Art*. He was an artist at the height of his powers, attracting major commissions for sculptures and architectural decorations. All the more extraordinary, then, that he should have wanted "to be known as an art-worker and not by the more restricted title of sculptor." After its successful inclusion in the Arts and Crafts Society exhibition of 1896, the screen went back to its commissioner, Alice Radcliffe, a London-based collector. When she died her collection passed to Alice Henderson, a Bath resident, who in turn left it to the Gallery. This was one of the most important bequests in the Gallery's history.

The Watersplash about 1899

By Henry La Thangue 1859-1929
Oil on canvas 117 x 94 cm

Given by Alice Dorothea Henderson 1954

Although of different generations, the painters of these two pictures were both concerned by the disappearance of traditional English rural life, La Thangue depicting farm workers in the fields, whilst Spencer got them to sit for portraits. In their different ways, they both treated their subjects with honesty and dignity.

The Watersplash transports us so successfully to a place of sunny, rural tranquillity that it is hard to believe what a radical painting it was in its time. Victorian taste dictated that artists should use fine brushes to give a porcelain-like finish to their pictures. By way of contrast, La Thangue used square hog's hair brushes to create a richly textured surface, focusing on movement and light rather than detail. Clearly, such painterly methods offended those who looked to art for refinement, but La Thangue was a British Impressionist who studied in France where he learnt the technique of painting in the open air. Returning to Britain, after failing to convert the Royal Academy to the new style, he joined a rival body, the New English Art Club. They advocated painting everyday subjects as spontaneously and naturally as possible.

Portrait of a Youth 1925

By Gilbert Spencer 1893-1979
Oil on canvas

Given by J. L. Behrend 1934

In 1898 La Thangue found his perfect rural retreat at Graffham near Petworth in Sussex, whereas Spencer was a native of Cookham in Berkshire. The title *Watersplash* refers to a shallow stream or ford crossing a road. In the picture, a flock of 34 geese are being driven forwards by a boy carrying a stick. The painting was bought by Alice Radcliffe in 1913 for £507. She left it to Miss Henderson of Bathwick, who in turn gave it to the Gallery in 1954. *Portrait of a youth* was a gift from J.L. Behrend, the man who ten years earlier had commissioned the Burghclere Chapel murals from Gilbert's more famous brother, Stanley.

William Harbutt 1911

By Edwin Whitney-Smith 1880-1952

Bronze 68 x 54 x 46 cm

Bequeathed by Elizabeth Cambridge Harbutt 1930

Anyone who has childhood memories of playing with Plasticine – the modelling material that could be worked and re-worked indefinitely – may be surprised to learn that it was both invented and manufactured in Bath. William Harbutt (1844-1921), who hailed from Newcastle, moved to Bath in 1874 to work as headmaster at Bath School of Art. An eminently practical man who enjoyed solving problems, Harbutt got frustrated with the way clay tended to dry up when left exposed to the elements. Aiming to create a replacement that would be oil- rather than water-based, Harbutt eventually came up with a material he called Plasticine. He made the discovery in the basement of his Bath home, 15 Alfred Street, and then enlisted his six children to help produce large enough quantities for use in his art school. In 1897 he began to supply local art shops with the material.

By 1900, demand had grown to such an extent that he decided to buy the old mill in Bathampton, two miles outside Bath, for use as a manufactory. The marketing of Plasticine as a children's toy boosted its circulation, with the result that it became a household name in Britain, besides being exported to over fifty other countries. The factory was run as a family business until 1983, when it finally closed down.

This bust of a very thoughtful-looking William Harbutt was made by his pupil, Edwin Whitney-Smith. Appropriately, he modelled the head in Plasticine before having it cast in bronze, which only goes to show how much respect the modelling material commanded in the artistic world before it came to be seen as a toy. The bust was bequeathed to the Gallery by William Harbutt's wife, Elizabeth, nine years after his death from pneumonia while on a business trip to New York.

Small harbour scene 1919

By Paul Klee 1879-1940

Oil, pen and pencil on paper attached to board 24 x 19 cm

Bequeathed by Lutz Haber 2008

This jewel-like painting, the most significant work of art acquired by the Gallery in recent years, tells an extraordinary story. It was painted in Munich by the Swiss artist Paul Klee, shortly after he was demobbed from the German army. Materials were still very scarce, so Klee recycled two older works – a drawing and a painting – to use as a backing for the new painting. He was in mid-career and just on the cusp of international stardom. Before the war, he belonged to the Blue Rider group of Expressionist painters who were inspired by tribal and children's art as well as the creations of the insane. Although initially ridiculed, by the 1920s the Expressionists were viewed as pioneers of modern art, a situation that unfortunately led to their works being branded as degenerate under the Nazis.

Despite its innocuous subject matter and joyful handling of colour, *Small harbour scene* narrowly avoided being lost for ever. Its first owner, Alfred Mayer, was nearly bankrupted by the hyper-inflation that crippled Germany during 1921-23. Forced to sell his collection, he passed the Klee to an old friend, Charlotte Haber, who hung it in the nursery of her young son, Lutz. The Habers were a Jewish family, and even though Lutz's father, a distinguished chemist, had converted to Christianity in the 1890s, this did not prevent him from losing his job in 1933. Charlotte fled with the children to Switzerland and then, in 1936, to London, managing to take the Klee with her because it was so small. When war broke out three years later, Lutz was interned as an enemy alien and temporarily deported to Canada. After hostilities ended, he managed to acquire British citizenship and eventually moved to Bath, the Klee never leaving his side. It was as if the picture became a talisman of the family's struggle to survive.

Reverse side of Small harbour scene showing a fragment of a male portrait

The Dressmakers about 1931

By William Roberts 1895-1980
Oil on canvas 51 x 41 cm
Given by the Contemporary Art Society 1944

Whereas Roberts was a great observer of human behaviour, finding his subjects in everyday situations, his near contemporary John Armstrong turned to the Classics, the Bible and the circus for inspiration. Influenced by Cubism, Roberts liked to pack his figures into tight spaces and reduce them to geometric shapes. Armstrong, on the other hand, took his cue from the Surrealists by favouring scenes with a timeless, dreamlike quality. His skeletal rower and five hunched companions are in the process of ferrying Psyche across the River Styx, which in mythology separated the world of the living from that of the dead. To enhance the other-worldly aura, the artist has used egg tempera pigments, which are more difficult to work with than oil paints and yield more subdued colours.

Psyche on the Styx 1927

By John Armstrong 1893-1973
Tempera on board 64 x 36 cm
Given by the Contemporary Art Society 1965

Roberts' dressmakers, on the other hand, have none of the frigid, statuesque quality of Psyche and her companions. Instead we see a group of well-fed women who are all writhing arms and legs as they cut and pin bits of material according to the latest dress patterns. The artist could not resist echoing their movements in the bunch of flowers displayed behind them. Roberts' more prosaic subjects reflect his humble origins, for he was a carpenter's son from Hackney who left school at 14 to serve a commercial apprenticeship. After attending evening art classes he won a scholarship to the Slade School of Art. Before war service intervened, he exhibited in 1915 with the Vorticist group, whose semi-abstract pictures celebrated modern industry.

The canal bridge, Sydney Gardens, Bath about 1927

By John Nash 1893-1977
Oil on canvas 71 x 76 cm
Purchased 1931

John Nash saw active service on the Western Front and went 'over the top' on 30 December 1917. The action, he said, "was pure murder and I was lucky to escape untouched." The following year he became an Official War Artist and painted his first major war painting, *Oppy Wood*, in a former herb-drying shed near Gerrard's Cross. Returning to civilian life after the Armistice was difficult enough for men from other backgrounds, however young artists such as Nash must have felt they had lost much of their pre-war momentum. Completely self-taught, he rarely visited galleries and looked instead to the countryside for inspiration. He depicted it as a place of harmony and tranquillity, untouched by the destruction that he had witnessed. Figures seldom populated his landscapes, and the group of pictures he made following a visit to Bath in 1925 were no exception.

The bridge at the centre of this canvas still exists in Sydney Gardens, which were originally laid out in the 1790s as commercial pleasure gardens. It was not long, however, before this romantic setting was changed forever by the industrial revolution, first of all in the form of engineer John Rennie's Kennet and Avon Canal of 1796-1810, which sliced through the park. Later, a second cutting and tunnels were dug for the Great Western Railway line, conceived by Isambard Kingdom Brunel in 1835 and opened in 1840. Although Nash's picture is one of the few urban views he ever painted, it makes no virtue of the industrial trappings. On the contrary, the trees in full summer foliage that flank the canal evoke a strong sense of nature's capacity for renewal in the face of change. The scene looks much the same today, for the Kennet and Avon Canal has been fully restored and walkers can follow the towpath all the way from Bath to Reading.

The canal, Sydney Gardens, Bath
by John Nash, watercolour

Roses in a blue vase about 1929

By Matthew Smith 1879-1959
Oil on canvas 60 x 45 cm

Purchased with the aid of the MLA / V&A Purchase Grant Fund, 1980

Most modern British artists born towards the end of the 19th century would generally leapfrog Impressionism and experiment instead with Cubism, abstraction or Surrealism. However, the palette of bright, anarchic colours pioneered in France by Henri Matisse and the Fauves (meaning 'wild beasts') from 1905 attracted limited following on British soil. With one notable exception – Matthew Arnold Bracy Smith, son of a Halifax wire manufacturer. The stuffy Victorian household in which he grew up did little to encourage his artistic leanings. He persevered nonetheless, being allowed to attend Manchester School of Art only on the condition that he did not draw from the nude. In 1905 he progressed to the Slade School of Art in London, followed three years later by a brief spell at Matisse's school in Paris.

Of delicate health and a distinctly nervous disposition, Smith looked more like a bank manager than the bohemian artist he eventually became. Much of his career was spent working in the South of France, where the dazzling Mediterranean light and radiant colours encouraged him to respond with thick, rhythmic brushstrokes that seemed to pulse with life. When he was not painting nudes and landscapes, he set up still lifes in his studio comprising flowers, fruit, ornaments and vivid drapes. *Roses in a blue vase* is a riot of pure colour and energy, with hardly any white mixed into the pigments. It seems extraordinary that a man so diffident and retiring should not only have nurtured such a passionate disposition, but also discovered the means to let rip in such swaggering style. He was knighted in 1954 and his gifts as a colourist were saluted by the young artist, Francis Bacon: "painting today is pure intuition and luck ... and in this game of chance Matthew Smith seems to have the gods on his side."

London Street looking towards Walcot, Bath about 1940

By Walter Sickert 1860-1942, assisted by Thérèse Lessore 1884-1945
Oil on canvas 48 x 79 cm

Purchased with the aid of the MLA / V&A Purchase Grant Fund, the Heritage Lottery Fund and the Friends of the Victoria Art Gallery, 2005

Sickert spent many years on the Continent and became friendly with the Impressionists. He despised academic painting, stating that his mission was to take art out of the drawing room and into the kitchen. After moving to London in 1905, he quickly formed a group of like-minded young painters, urging them to tackle working class street scenes and interiors. Later he set up his own etching school and studio, where he was assisted by Thérèse Lessore, his future wife. He himself loved the half-light, so much so that he would blur his sitter's features if that was what he actually saw. During 1917-18 and 1938-42 he moved to Bath to escape the London air raids. He adored the slightly seedy and soiled Georgian architecture, and the way the streets seemed to stretch effortlessly into the surrounding hills.

From 1938 Sickert lived with his third wife, Thérèse, in Bathampton, two miles from Bath, where a shared grave preserves their memory. He got involved with the artistic life of the city, opening shows at this Gallery and offering his services gratis as a teacher at the Bath School of Art. His advanced age meant that he needed assistance in the studio, so he dispatched Thérèse to take photographs of the Bath buildings he wanted to paint. Though a good painter in her own right, she was mindful of her husband's frailty and carried out her tasks willingly, squaring up the photographs to transfer the view onto paper first, and then with his approval onto canvas. The ultimate aim was to retain the freshness of the moment the scene was first glimpsed. This painting is a view of London Street taken from the iron railings outside St Swithin's Church. The combination of light traffic and limpid, late afternoon sunshine makes for a seductive image.

The Reflective Horse, Stall Street, Bath 1940
by Thérèse Lessore, oil on canvas

All Saints Chapel, Bath, after the Blitz 1942

By Leslie Atkinson 1911-2004
Gouache on board 59 x 95 cm
Given by the artist 1980

Over two consecutive nights in late April 1942, Bath was attacked by German bombers flying in three waves, resulting in massive destruction and the loss of over 400 lives. As Bath had no military targets worth speaking of, the city was unprepared and undefended. The purpose of this raid and others like it was to inflict severe damage on cities with large numbers of historic buildings, thus undermining civilian morale. Such attacks came to be known as Baedeker raids, the term being borrowed from a series of popular pre-war travel books. In Bath, many churches were ruined, including All Saints Chapel just below Lansdown Crescent. Built in the Gothic style by John Palmer in 1794, the chapel took a direct hit from a bomb that blew out two sections of wall. The roof and fittings were then consumed in the ensuing fire.

Three days after the raid, the Official War Artist John Piper was sent to Bath to make a record of the devastation. He found it a deeply harrowing experience.

While working on a painting of the chapel, he discovered another artist sitting nearby, sketching the same subject. This second artist was Leslie Atkinson, who worked in the Admiralty's camouflage unit that had been relocated to Bath. Atkinson had been on a reconnaissance flight over Scotland when Bath was blitzed, but on hearing the terrible news he rushed back to the city. Despite having no official brief, he managed to produce half a dozen paintings and drawings of the wreckage, executed with the care and assurance one would expect from someone who had studied under Eric Ravilious and John Nash (see p. 53). In the immediate aftermath of the bombings, many of those who fled their homes took refuge in the same caves whence the stone had been dug to create the city's Georgian buildings.

The Baedeker raids were primarily in reprisal for our destruction of the almost complete wooden medieval Baltic city of Lübeck during the bombing of U-boat pens there.

People in the wind 1950

By Kenneth Armitage 1916-2002
Bronze 65 x 40 x 34 cm

Purchased with the aid of the Heritage Lottery Fund, the Art Fund, the MLA / V&A Purchase Grant Fund and the Friends of the Victoria Art Gallery, 1999

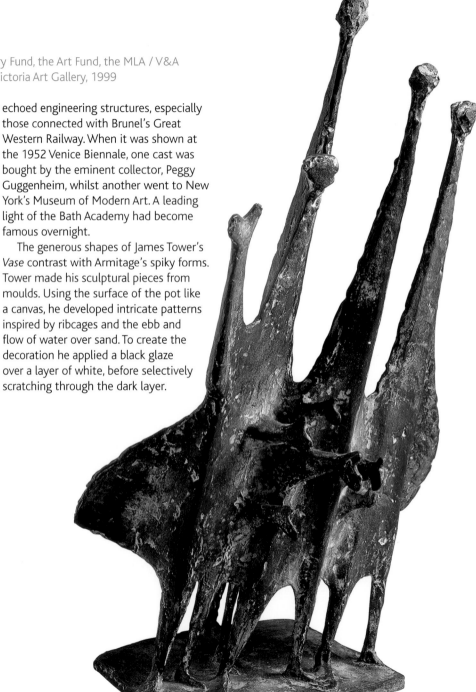

After Bath School of Art was destroyed during the Bath Blitz, it moved into temporary premises for four years until the principal, Clifford Ellis, relocated the School to Corsham Court in Wiltshire, courtesy of Lord Methuen. From 1946 the School was renamed the Bath Academy of Art. As Head of Sculpture, Kenneth Armitage delighted in the spacious facilities and took a studio in Corsham so that he could combine teaching with studio practice. His colleague James Tower set up a pottery in the old stables and taught ceramics at the Academy from 1949-64.

Armitage described the event that inspired *People in the wind*: "looking out of the window on a very windy day I saw a woman walking, holding two children, all three leaning against the wind, and this gave me an idea: I started making tiny maquettes with figures with long necks." Noting also that: "If you look at a crowd ... you just see odd arms swinging and the odd leg moving", he decided to meld his figures into one mass. The sculpture was modelled in wire mesh and plaster and cast in bronze. Its streamlined shapes echoed engineering structures, especially those connected with Brunel's Great Western Railway. When it was shown at the 1952 Venice Biennale, one cast was bought by the eminent collector, Peggy Guggenheim, whilst another went to New York's Museum of Modern Art. A leading light of the Bath Academy had become famous overnight.

The generous shapes of James Tower's *Vase* contrast with Armitage's spiky forms. Tower made his sculptural pieces from moulds. Using the surface of the pot like a canvas, he developed intricate patterns inspired by ribcages and the ebb and flow of water over sand. To create the decoration he applied a black glaze over a layer of white, before selectively scratching through the dark layer.

Vase 1983

By James Tower 1919-88
Tin-glazed earthenware 37 x 49 x 16 cm

Purchased with the aid of the MLA / V&A Purchase Grant Fund
and the Friends of the Victoria Art Gallery, 2004

Sun up 1960

By Gillian Ayres 1930-
Oil on canvas 122 x 92 cm

Purchased with the aid of the Art Fund, the MLA / V&A Purchase Grant Fund
and the Friends of the Victoria Art Gallery, 2011

During the 1950s and 1960s, the Bath Academy of Art established itself as one of the best art schools in the country, thanks to the visionary leadership of Clifford Ellis. He brought in scores of young, cutting edge artists from London and St Ives to spend a couple of days a week teaching at the Academy, which was then based in Corsham. Gillian Ayres was on the staff of the Academy from 1959 to 1965, working alongside such luminaries as Robyn Denny, Adrian Heath and Howard Hodgkin. Ayres's teaching programme was based on a syllabus devised some years previously by William Scott, but her approach was not to teach according to set formulae. Instead she developed a more student-oriented style, a prototype in fact of the tutorial system still in use today, whereby students are encouraged to follow their own lines of creative investigation.

Sun Up, which dates from the artist's Corsham period, shows that the flair she extended to her teaching duties was an equally prominent feature of her painting practice. Here she has combined vigorous brushwork and the throwing of pigment at the canvas with the free use of turpentine as a colour thinner, allowing the paint to stain, dribble and splatter. The effect is to convey a sense of day chasing night, of clarity of shape and colour gradually supplanting darkness and obscurity.

Ayres's use of 'atmospherics' in paintings such as this one could be traced to her interest in J.M.W. Turner's work and the theories of the Sublime propounded by Edmund Burke and Immanuel Kant. In order to test the theories, she made frequent visits to Cader Idris in North Wales, noting especially the way mist and vapour could just as quickly cloak or reveal the underlying terrain. *Sun Up* is informed by her awareness of such natural phenomena.

Daisy Fairy 1981-82

By Peter Blake 1932-

Oil on board 28 x 17 cm

Purchased with the aid of the Art Fund, the MLA / V&A Purchase Grant Fund and the Friends of the Victoria Art Gallery, 2007

It might bear the name of Blake's second daughter, Daisy, born in 1974, but this exquisitely painted picture is not a portrait of her. Like many of Blake's paintings, *Daisy Fairy* was based on a photograph clipped from a magazine, the act of selection transforming something ephemeral into something enduring. As a Pop artist in the 1950s and 1960s, he had taken a similar approach with his depictions of film-stars and popular music icons. He achieved widespread fame in 1967 with his iconic cover for The Beatles' album, 'Sergeant Pepper's Lonely Hearts Club Band', which he created with his first wife, Jann Haworth. After the birth of their first child, the intensity of life in London began to take its toll, so they decided to move to the country. In 1969, Blake bought the recently decommissioned Wellow railway station near Bath and set up his studio in the signal box.

Although this rural interlude lasted ten years, they were not solitary ones. In March 1975 Blake formed an association with six other artists who had moved to the countryside, calling themselves the Brotherhood of Ruralists. They aspired to "the continuation of a certain kind of English painting; we admire Samuel Palmer, Stanley Spencer ... English landscape, the Pre-Raphaelites, etc. ... our aims are to paint about love, beauty, joy, sentiment and magic. We still believe in painting with oil paint on canvas, putting the picture in a frame and, hopefully, that someone will like it, buy it and hang it on their wall to enjoy." At Wellow, Blake took a new interest in narrative and literary subjects, including a major series of fairy paintings that appeared innocent and knowing, both flesh and fantasy. *Daisy Fairy* was painted for his 1981 Tate retrospective and presented in an old, exotic frame that he had picked up in a junk shop or market-stall.

Lady-hare on dog 1999

By Sophie Ryder 1963-
Bronze 152 x 175 x 48 cm

Purchased with the aid of the MLA / V&A Purchase Grant Fund
and the Friends of the Victoria Art Gallery, 2000

As a child, Sophie Ryder already loved drawing and making things, especially characters she could weave into a story. When aged ten she was distressed on hearing the news of Picasso's death, and it would be tempting to imagine she saw his preoccupation with that mythic being, the minotaur, as his enduring legacy. Certainly the major theme in the work of this Cotswolds-based artist has been the creation of "characters beyond animal form." In other words, while her ultimate concern is to explore what it means to be human and to interact with other living creatures, she feels she would fall at the first hurdle if her works were simply portraits. Hybridising the human form with bulls and hares gives her figures greater universality.

Ryder's work first drew attention in 1984 when her degree show at the Royal Academy included quarter life-size wire sculptures of a jumbo jet and a London bus. For years to come, wire remained her material of choice, although the pieces did sometimes rust when left out-of-doors. Bronze, on the other hand, could be fully weather-proofed, so Ryder started to work in this material. Her habit of embedding recycled machinery and toys into her surfaces gave the bronze-casters quite a headache. *Lady-hare on dog* was acquired following a hugely successful indoor and outdoor exhibition of Ryder's work that we mounted in 1999. The piece is so loved by visitors that the nose of the dog has become shiny through repeated rubbing.

The figure of the lady-hare is a quasi self-portrait, invented by the artist to act as consort to the minotaur. In this sculpture, however, she has found another companion, dog, to share in her adventures. It is a reconciliation of opposites, for the hare is of course the traditional quarry of this type of dog.

Silence 1997-2004

By Howard Hodgkin 1932-
Oil on wood 47 x 47 cm

Purchased with the aid of the Art Fund and the Friends of the Victoria
Art Gallery, 2008

When the critic John Ruskin accused James Abbot McNeil Whistler of "flinging a pot of paint in the public's face", the latter explained that the brushstrokes and colours of any single painting were informed by a lifetime of experience. This statement could equally be applied to Howard Hodgkin, who studied at the Camberwell School of Art and the Bath Academy of Art, before going on to teach at the Academy from 1955-66. But there is one very important difference – the seeming spontaneity of Hodgkin's work is the end product of a prolonged struggle, each action being dependent on extensive thought, contemplation and self-criticism. His paint surfaces are built up in layers over years, and will often be completely reworked more than once before the finished piece is released from the studio.

Silence is no exception to this rule, for when it was first exhibited in 1997 it looked completely different. Technique aside, however, it is natural to want to know what the picture means. Hodgkin remains infuriatingly reticent about the events that inspire his pictures. They are always very personal to him, comprising moments of profound feeling, and he is only satisfied when the marks of his brushes finally succeed in recapturing the primal emotional charge. The title is the only clue we are given, for he prefers that we should weave our own stories around his allusive paintings, starting with the sense of space and light conjured by the layers of pigment.

Silence, like all his paintings, was painted on a piece of recycled wood, in this case the back of a 17th-century Dutch frame. True to its title, it evokes an almost mesmeric sense of stillness. The broad tonal range, moving from glowing orange to near black, seems suggestive of the mystery associated with the half light.

New discoveries

These two works on paper entered the Gallery's collection more than 60 years ago and were catalogued as originals by Homer and Vlaminck, names that now embody huge commercial, academic and popular status. Investigations into the Vlaminck are ongoing and, whilst not wanting to prejudge the outcome, the facts as we know them do not rule out a positive attribution. The watercolour was purchased for £28 following its loan to an exhibition of modern French and British pictures held in the Pump Room in Bath over the winter of 1937-38. The artist was still very much alive and working prolifically, the price paid was not unreasonable for the time, and it seems unlikely that Vlaminck's recent work would have been deemed worthy of forgery quite so soon.

The provenance of the 'Homer' can likewise be traced back to the artist's lifetime. It was given to the Gallery in 1946 by Katharine Kimball (1866-1949), an American printmaker and resident of Bath for 27 years. Kimball's own manuscript catalogue of her collection states that the drawing was given to her by Mr E. W. Rollins when she was a pupil at Miss Newhall's School in Boston in 1881. Kimball was very punctilious and would have been concerned to record her memories accurately, in anticipation of her entire collection of over 300 items being left to the Gallery.

Ox cart in the state of Maine about 1875

Attributed to Winslow Homer 1836-1910
Pencil and gouache 16 x 21 cm
Given by Katharine Kimball 1946

Road through a village

Attributed to Maurice de Vlaminck 1876-1958

Gouache 46 x 55 cm

Purchased 1938

Further information

The Gallery welcomes enquiries about its collections and requests to view items that may not be on display. Searching the collections on line is possible via our website (www.victoriagal.org.uk) and the Your Paintings site created by the Public Catalogue Foundation with the BBC (www.bbc.co.uk/arts/yourpaintings). For a complete visual survey of the Gallery's oil paintings in printed format see *Oil Paintings in Public Ownership in Somerset*, Public Catalogue Foundation, 2008.

Information on accessing paintings from the Gallery's collection that are displayed in the Pump Room, Assembly Rooms and Guildhall in Bath can be found on the internet (www.romanbaths.co.uk, www.fashionmuseum.co.uk and www.bathvenues.co.uk/guildhall.aspx).

Acknowledgements

I must pay tribute to the huge effort that Katharine Wall and the Gallery's collections team have put into information retrieval over the last decade. This has included the reassembling of data that was lost or buried, as well as the creation of a collections database containing details and images of 12,000 objects. I am also indebted to the many volunteers who have helped with the sorting, cleaning and listing of objects, giving so generously of their time and expertise. The Gallery's pre-20th-century foreign paintings were exhaustively researched and catalogued by Susan Steer, who identified the creator and first owner of *The death of Cleopatra* (p. 9).

The local community has made a vital contribution towards acquisitions for the Gallery's collection via our charitable arm, the Friends of the Victoria Art Gallery. When added to the amounts Bath & North East Somerset Council invests from its own purchase fund, these locally sourced monies count as the partnership element that encourages larger national funders to lend their support. Scanning the pages of this book, readers will note the frequency with which the Art Fund, the MLA/V&A Purchase Grant Fund and the National Lottery are mentioned, to all of whom we owe an enormous debt. Similarly, without the Council's backing, it would have been impossible to save many of the works of art illustrated in this book.

We would like to thank Gillian Ayres, Peter Blake, Howard Hodgkin and Sophie Ryder for their permission to reproduce for free the images that appear in this guide. Other copyright holders who have kindly granted permission are Annette Armstrong, Alice Kadel, Julia Gibson and Maureen Tower (pp. 51, 55, 59 and 61 respectively). Images are also reproduced with the permission of the following: © the artist's estate/Bridgeman Art Library (ps. 45 and 51); © the Estate of John Nash / Bridgeman Art Library (p. 52); © the Estate of John David Roberts, reproduced with the permission of the William Roberts Society (p.50); © the Estate of Walter R. Sickert. All rights reserved, DACS 2011 (p. 56); © Henry & John Lessore (p.57); © Kenneth Armitage Foundation / Bridgeman Art Library (p. 60). Every effort has been made to seek permission to reproduce those images whose copyright does not reside with the Victoria Art Gallery. Any omissions are entirely unintentional, and the details should be addressed to the publishers.

Jonathan Benington, Manager
Victoria Art Gallery
Bath & North East Somerset Council